GOD CREATED the ANIMALS of the World

Written and Illustrated by
EARL and BONITA SNELLENBERGER

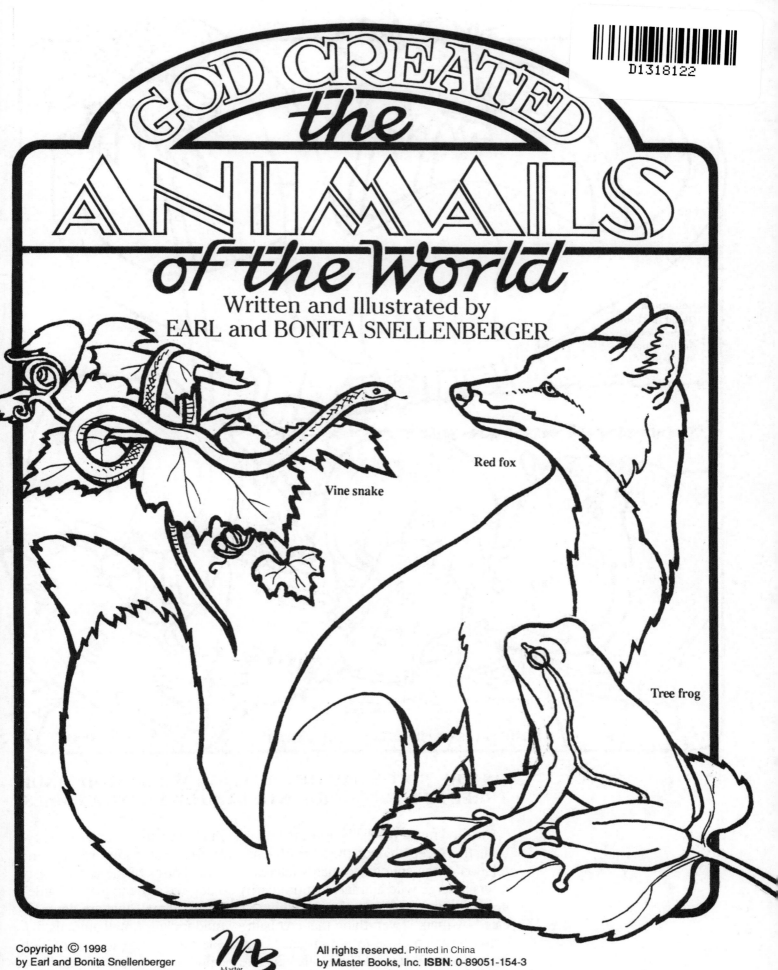

Vine snake

Red fox

Tree frog

Master Books

D1318122

Behemoths
(Read the Bible's description of the behemoth in Job 40:15-24.)

Hippopotamuses

SOME PAIRS OF "BEASTS OF THE EARTH"

Rhinoceroses

ON THE SIXTH DAY OF CREATION WEEK, GOD MADE THREE DIFFERENT GROUPS OF LAND DWELLING ANIMALS.

"And God made (1) the beast of the earth . . . and (2) cattle . . . and (3) everything that creepeth upon the earth" (Genesis 1:25) — categories based on the relation of the animals to man's interests. Thus, "beasts of the earth" likely refers to large wild animals that ordinarily do not live close to man. "Cattle" here truly means *livestock*, and likely refers to all animals that are domesticated by man. "Everything that creepeth" would include small animals that crawl or creep close to the ground. God made a male and female of each animal, mates that would have offspring like themselves — "after their kind."

Camels

Goats

Cattle

SOME PAIRS OF "CATTLE" KINDS

SOME PAIRS OF "CREEPING THINGS" WITH ADAM

Chameleons

Toads

Chipmunks

AFTER MAKING PAIRS OF EACH ANIMAL KIND, GOD MADE ADAM, THE FIRST MAN, IN HIS OWN IMAGE.

Man is God's very special creation, superior to all animal life on earth. "And God said, Let *us* [Father, Son, and Holy Spirit] make man in *our* image, after *our* likeness" God is three persons, yet He is one — for "God created man in *His* own image" (Gen. 1:26-27). Both animals and men have physical bodies made of the earth's elements and both have souls (or consciousness). But unlike the animals, only Adam was created with an *immortal* spirit — having a beginning and then going on forever. The spirit of an animal no longer exists when its body dies and goes back to the earth (Eccl. 3:21).

God gave the hairy animals that we call *mammals* warm-bloodedness, the ability to maintain a relatively stable body temperature while the temperature of the environment varies over a wide range. Man certainly is *not* an animal, even though he has a body like a mammal.

Both men and animals were originally vegetarians. Read Gen. 1:29-31.

ADAM NAMED ALL THE PAIRS OF ANIMALS, BUT HE WAS ALONE UNTIL GOD MADE A SUITABLE BRIDE FOR HIM.

God brought the animals He had made to Adam so the man could give them names (Gen. 2:19). As all of the pairs of animals passed before Adam for naming, he realized that no real fellowship was possible between him and them. He was truly alone. Adam was so completely unlike the animals in intelligence and spirituality, no suitable companion and helper for him could be found among them. "And the Lord God said, It is not good that the man should be alone" (Gen. 2:18). Then God formed a woman, named Eve, out of Adam's side, a helper like him — the perfect bride for the perfect groom.

God planted the beautiful Garden of Eden to be the home of Adam and Eve (Gen. 2:8).

GOD MADE ADAM AND EVE THE EARTH'S STEWARDS, TO CARE FOR ANIMALS — ALL OF WHICH WERE PLANT-EATERS.

God established mankind as His stewards over the created world, and to "have dominion over . . . every living thing that moveth upon the earth" (Gen. 1:26-28). As they began their stewardship, using the earth for good under the direction of God, Adam and Eve must have enjoyed the gentle animals God made — all of which, like them, lived on a vegetarian diet (Gen. 1:29, 30). Some of the animals God created are those known today as *mammals*. Mammals are warm-blooded, and are the only animals that possess true hair and produce milk with which they feed their young.

5

Eve with pigmy shrew

Indricotherium

African elephant

Fossils, the hardened remains of living things buried by flood waters, show that lush plant life — abundant food for all — once grew on earth from pole to pole.

GOD MADE MANY, MANY DIFFERENT KINDS OF MAMMALS, BOTH LARGE AND SMALL.

The largest mammal known ever to walk the earth was the monstrous *Indricotherium* (in-DRI-coe-THEE-ree-um). It stood 18 feet (5.4 meters) high at the shoulders — able to eat leaves from the topmost branches of trees. The record for the largest mammal living on earth today was a male African elephant that stood over 12½ feet tall (3.66 meters) and weighed 22,000 pounds (9,979 kilograms). God also made little mammals, and the smallest one in the world is the pygmy white-toothed shrew. Fully grown, this tiny creature weighs only 2 g (1/14 oz). Truly, God's creation is amazing!

The extinct Eryops was 7 feet (2.13 meters) long. Common amphibians still living today — including frogs, toads, newts, and salamanders — are much smaller.

Hind legs develop first.

Front legs and lungs develop.

The tail shrinks, then disappears.

The young tadpole grows quickly.

Mass of eggs

THE GOD-DESIGNED METAMORPHOSIS OF THE FROG

Adult frog

Warty newt (male)

Eryops

Tiger salamander

GOD ALSO CREATED COLD-BLOODED ANIMALS KNOWN AS *AMPHIBIANS*, BOTH LARGE AND SMALL.

God made different kinds of amphibians, some of which are now extinct, such as the large *Eryops* (ER-ee-ops). Cold-blooded, an amphibian's body temperature is the same as the temperature of its surroundings. Amphibians, which have either smooth or warty skin, lay their jelly-covered eggs in water or very damp surroundings. The eggs hatch to become *larvae*, the early form of an animal, such as a frog. The larval frog is a *tadpole* with gills, like fish, to live in water. In a process called *metamorphosis*, the tadpole becomes a frog — having lungs for breathing air on land.

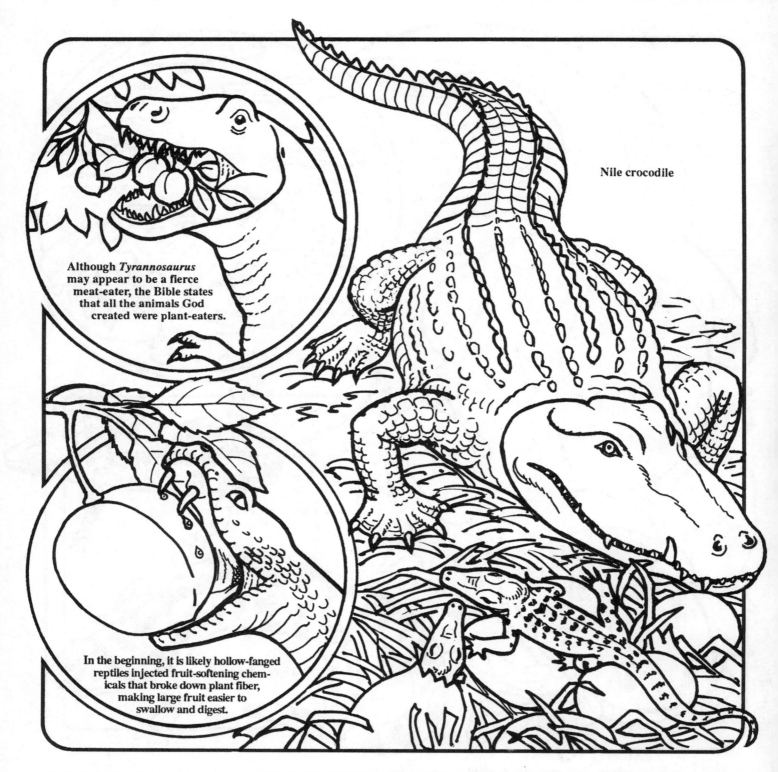

Nile crocodile

Although *Tyrannosaurus* may appear to be a fierce meat-eater, the Bible states that all the animals God created were plant-eaters.

In the beginning, it is likely hollow-fanged reptiles injected fruit-softening chemicals that broke down plant fiber, making large fruit easier to swallow and digest.

GOD MADE MANY, MANY DIFFERENT KINDS OF ANIMALS KNOWN AS *REPTILES*, BOTH LARGE AND SMALL.

Reptiles, like amphibians, are cold-blooded, but there are several important differences between them. Unlike amphibians, reptiles have dry, scaly skin, their eggs are enclosed in a tough, leathery shell, and they have clawed toes. The largest reptiles God created were among a group of creatures now considered to be extinct — the dinosaurs. In fact, only 4 of the 16 or 17 different groups of reptiles known to have existed remain today: (1) snakes and lizards, (2) turtles and tortoises, (3) crocodiles and alligators, and (4) the tuatara, a unique reptile in a group of its own (see page 27).

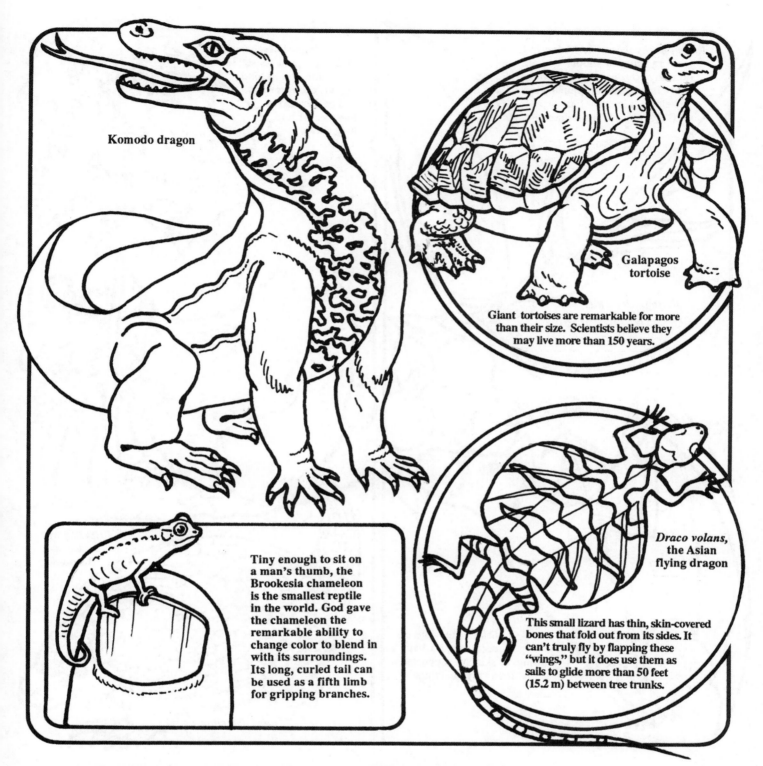

Komodo dragon

Galapagos tortoise

Giant tortoises are remarkable for more than their size. Scientists believe they may live more than 150 years.

Tiny enough to sit on a man's thumb, the Brookesia chameleon is the smallest reptile in the world. God gave the chameleon the remarkable ability to change color to blend in with its surroundings. Its long, curled tail can be used as a fifth limb for gripping branches.

Draco volans, the Asian flying dragon

This small lizard has thin, skin-covered bones that fold out from its sides. It can't truly fly by flapping these "wings," but it does use them as sails to glide more than 50 feet (15.2 m) between tree trunks.

THE REPTILES GOD CREATED VARY GREATLY IN KIND AND SIZE AND LIVE IN VERY DIFFERENT PLACES.

The Komodo dragon, exceeding 10 feet (3.5 meters) in length, is thought to be the largest true lizard that has ever lived on land. Limited to living on a few remote, uninhabited Indonesian islands, the Komodo dragon was only discovered in 1912. A tortoise is a land turtle with elephant-like legs, and the giant tortoises of the Galapagos Islands are the world's largest, weighing as much as 600 pounds (272 kg). These peaceful plant-eaters feed upon thorny giant cacti. Unlike the earthbound Komodo dragon and the Galapagos tortoise, the Asian flying dragon sails among the treetops.

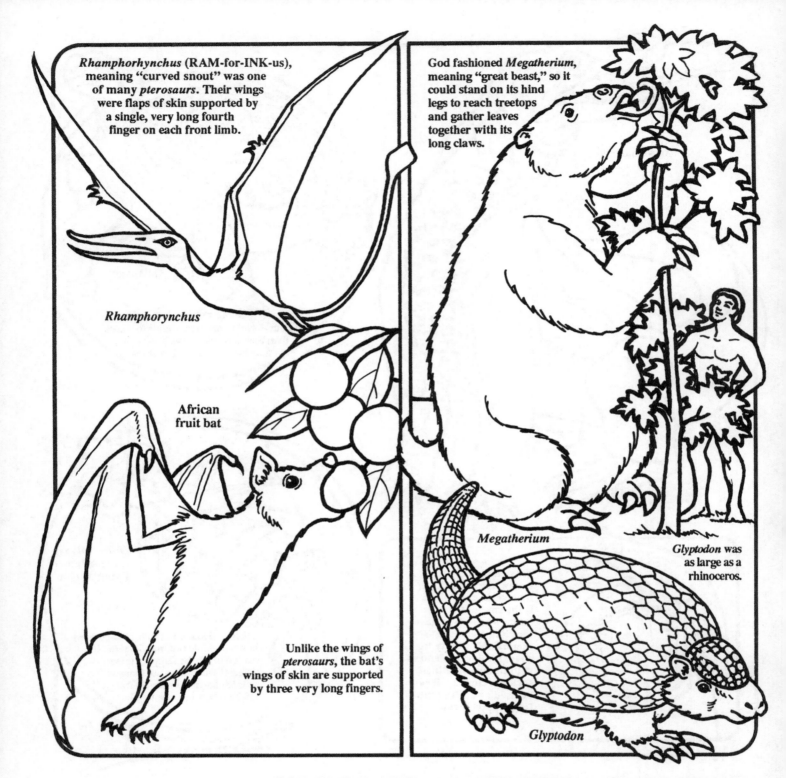

Rhamphorhynchus (RAM-for-INK-us), meaning "curved snout" was one of many *pterosaurs*. Their wings were flaps of skin supported by a single, very long fourth finger on each front limb.

Rhamphorynchus

African fruit bat

Unlike the wings of *pterosaurs*, the bat's wings of skin are supported by three very long fingers.

God fashioned *Megatherium,* meaning "great beast," so it could stand on its hind legs to reach treetops and gather leaves together with its long claws.

Megatherium

Glyptodon was as large as a rhinoceros.

Glyptodon

GOD MADE ANIMALS WITH WINGS TO FLY ABOVE THE EARTH AND OTHERS TO LIVE ON THE EARTH'S SURFACE.

God did create reptiles with true wings known as *pterosaurs* (TER-eh-sores), meaning "winged lizards." Strong flyers, *pterosaurs* probably became extinct after the great flood of Noah's day. Today, a variety of bats, the only known flying mammal, live almost everywhere on earth. God created other mammals, now extinct, that were large, heavy, and earthbound. *Megatherium* (MEG-a-THEE-ree-um) was a giant ground sloth the size of an elephant with a long, flexible tongue for stripping tasty leaves from branches. The huge *Glyptodon* was covered with plates of massive, bony armor.

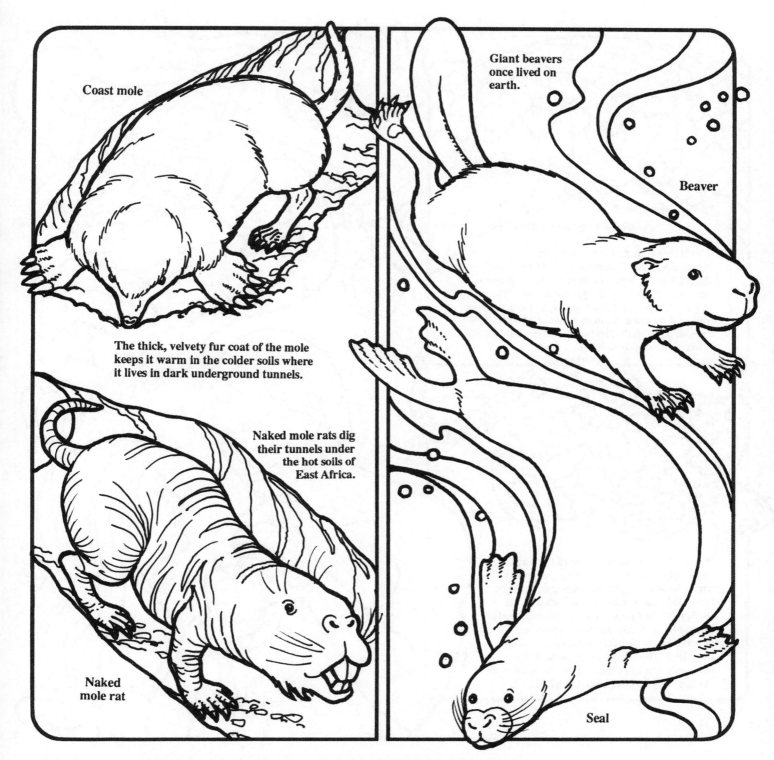

Coast mole

The thick, velvety fur coat of the mole keeps it warm in the colder soils where it lives in dark underground tunnels.

Naked mole rats dig their tunnels under the hot soils of East Africa.

Naked mole rat

Giant beavers once lived on earth.

Beaver

Seal

GOD MADE ANIMALS THAT ARE AT HOME BENEATH THE EARTH AND OTHERS THAT ARE AT HOME IN WATER.

God gave thick-furred moles stout, clawed front paws for swiftly digging long underground tunnels in hard soil — 12 to 15 feet (3.7 to 4.6 meters) in an hour. The naked mole rat digs its tunnels another way — with long front teeth that also are the right shape for nibbling on plant roots and bulbs. The beaver's paddle-like tail and webbed feet are perfect for swimming underwater much of the time. God gave seals sleek, tapered bodies and four strong flippers for a life in water. In fact, God gave every animal exactly what it needs to succeed — just where He decided it would live on earth.

11

Vestigial Legs on a Snake

The Hebrew word for serpent, *nachash*, originally meant "shining, upright creature" — that is, having legs — according to some Bible scholars. The vestigial legs, remnants of the past, of such snakes as the anaconda, boa constrictor, and python are a reminder to man of his fall — resulting in God's cursing the serpent above all other animals (Gen. 3:13).

"And the Lord God said unto the serpent, Because thou hast done this . . . upon thy belly shalt thou go." Falling upon the serpent, this curse was truly directed at the evil spirit that possessed the animal's body and used its throat to speak deceiving words, Satan — "that old serpent called the devil" (Rev. 12:9). It is possible for demonic spirits to indwell or "possess" both animal and human bodies (Luke 8:33).

GOD'S WORLD WAS "VERY GOOD" — PERFECT FOR ALL LIVING THINGS, INCLUDING ANIMALS, UNTIL MAN SINNED.

Satan, the evil, fallen angel, speaking through the serpent, deceived Eve. Then Adam sinned by eating of the tree of knowledge of good and evil against God's command. "Wherefore, as by one man sin entered into the world, and death by sin; and so death passed upon all men, for that all have sinned" (Romans 5:12). There was no death, conflict, or struggle for survival before Adam sinned; the finished creation was "very good" (Gen. 1:31). Because of Adam's sin, God brought the curse of death and decay not only upon Adam, but upon his dominion (Gen. 3:17-20; Rom. 8:20-22; Cor. 15:21, 22).

Jesus is called "the Lamb of God."

When Jesus was crucified, He became the innocent, sinless, and final sacrifice of God "which taketh away the sin of the world" (John 1:29). In contrast, the serpent, the physical representation of Satan, became a creature of loathing and dread, with some serpents' fangs degenerating into deadly weapons.

Just as the Bible says, the serpent truly eats dust (Gen.1:15), transferring dust from its forked tongue to an organ (Jacobson's) on the mouth's roof where sensory cells analyze its content and the environment.

Nostril
Heat-sensing pit
Sensory cells
Poison duct
Nasal passage
Jacobson's organ
Hollow fang
Extendable windpipe for breathing while feeding
Gripping teeth
Forked tongue used in scenting

GOD SAID TO THE DEVIL INHABITING THE SERPENT, "I WILL PUT ENMITY BETWEEN THEE AND THE WOMAN" (Gen. 3:15).

To prevent Satan from winning the loyalty of Eve and all her descendants, God put enmity, a deep-seated hatred, between them. And He began to redeem mankind — to save them from the state of sin and its consequences. God slew innocent animals to clothe Adam and Eve, showing them that an atonement (covering) for sin must be a blood sacrifice. One day, Satan would injure "the seed of the woman," Jesus Christ, at the cross. But Jesus triumphantly rose from the dead to deliver a mortal head wound to Satan, the serpent, who will be cast into a lake of fire (Gen. 3:15; Rev. 20:10).

God had shown mankind the need to make animal sacrifices, shedding blood on the altar as an atonement for sins until the day Jesus, the promised seed of the woman, died on the cross as the great sacrifice for sins forever.

THE RESULTS OF SIN WERE TERRIBLE. VIOLENCE, DEATH, AND THE STRUGGLE TO SURVIVE FILLED THE EARTH.

When the two sons of Adam and Eve made sacrifices for their sins, Abel slew the finest of his flock of sheep as the blood offering God required. When Cain's disobedient offering of the fruits of the ground was rejected, he violently killed his brother Abel in anger. The Bible doesn't tell us exactly when some animals began killing others in the fallen world, but it does say that "all flesh [that includes animals] had corrupted his way upon the earth" before the great flood (Gen. 6:11, 12). Carnivorous appetites and increasing hostility may have developed in animals soon after Adam's fall.

Spider monkey

Jamaican fruit bat

Yawning gorilla

Panda

THERE WERE SHARP-TOOTHED ANIMALS THAT REMAINED PLANT-EATERS, JUST AS THEY WERE IN THE BEGINNING.

As the degenerative influence of sin filled the earth, features that once helped some animals obtain and eat plant food, such as sharp teeth and claws, were used to kill and devour other living things in the fallen world. Still, the appearance of sharp teeth and claws can be deceiving and should not be cause to believe God originally designed some animals to be carnivorous. Spider monkeys, fruit bats, gorillas, and pandas have the physical characteristics of today's fierce, meat-eating animals, but they are all gentle plant-eaters, of no harm to other creatures.

15

Zebras' sensitive ears can twist in different directions to pick up faint sounds.

The African zebra's life is often threatened by hungry leopards, lions, wild dogs, and hyenas. However, God gave the zebra swift legs so it easily can outrun a predator over a long distance.

The sugar glider of Australia and New Guinea is a small mammal about the size of a chipmunk. When it dives from a high branch, the outstretched skin between its front and back legs act like a kite to carry it more than 150 feet (45.7 meters) between trees.

Sugar glider

Virginia opposum

When threatened, the opposum feigns death — it "plays possum" — until the predator loses interest and leaves.

WITH SIN IN THE WORLD, SOME ANIMALS BECAME PREDATORS; OTHER ANIMALS BECAME "ESCAPE ARTISTS."

Before the world was created, God knew it would be corrupted by sin, and He established a plan to renew it through Jesus Christ (Rev. 13:8). God also gave some animals the means to escape from others that became predators in the fallen world. Zebras have excellent senses — hearing, eyesight, and sense of smell — to detect lurking enemies and strong legs to run for safety before they attack. When the little sugar glider is threatened in its treetop home, it leaps into space and sails to safety in a distant tree on wing-like flaps of skin. Opposums simply "play dead" to escape from hungry enemies.

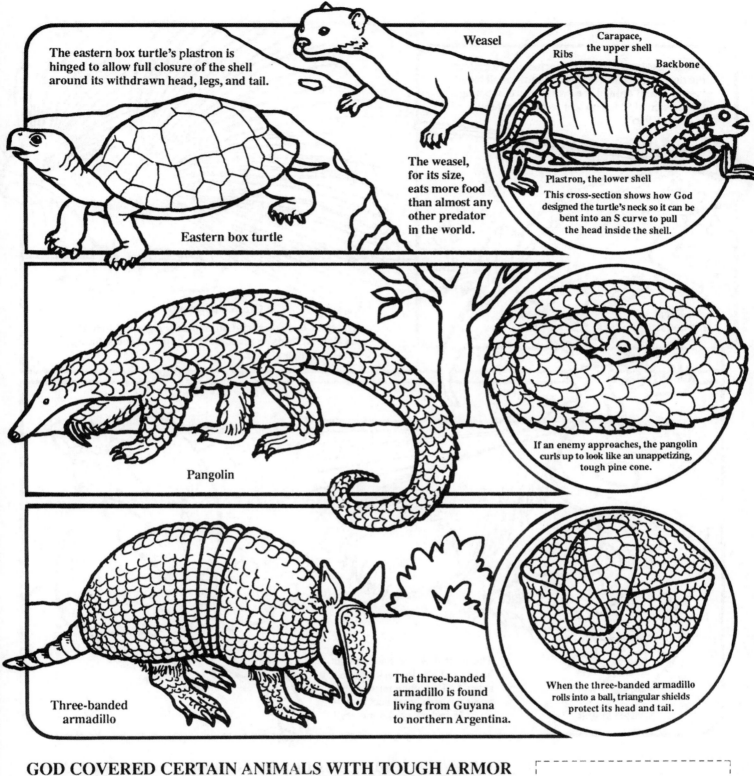

The eastern box turtle's plastron is hinged to allow full closure of the shell around its withdrawn head, legs, and tail.

Weasel

Ribs

Carapace, the upper shell

Backbone

Plastron, the lower shell

This cross-section shows how God designed the turtle's neck so it can be bent into an S curve to pull the head inside the shell.

Eastern box turtle

The weasel, for its size, eats more food than almost any other predator in the world.

Pangolin

If an enemy approaches, the pangolin curls up to look like an unappetizing, tough pine cone.

Three-banded armadillo

The three-banded armadillo is found living from Guyana to northern Argentina.

When the three-banded armadillo rolls into a ball, triangular shields protect its head and tail.

GOD COVERED CERTAIN ANIMALS WITH TOUGH ARMOR TO PROTECT THEM FROM FIERCE, HUNGRY PREDATORS.

Their meat would make a tasty meal, but God clothed slow turtles in hard shells. When threatened, turtles withdraw into their safe homes and wait until hungry enemies go away. The gentle African tree pangolin is slow-moving also, but it, too, is not easy prey. God covered the pangolin with hard, sharp, overlapping scales for protection. Each end of the three-banded armadillo's body is covered with tough, arched shields. These two shields are connected by three bony rings that serve as very flexible joints, allowing the armadillo to curl up into an almost invulnerable suit of armor.

17

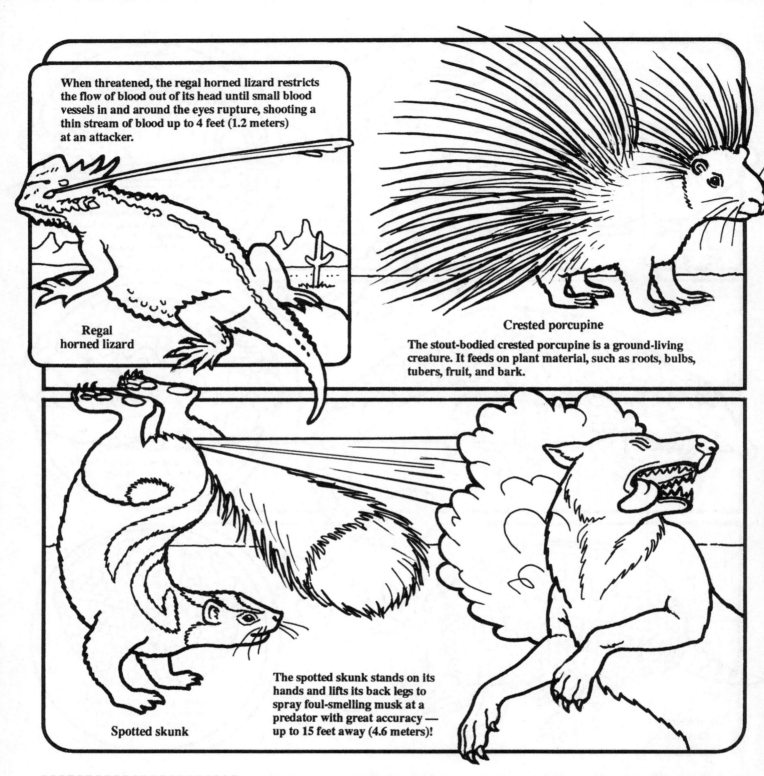

When threatened, the regal horned lizard restricts the flow of blood out of its head until small blood vessels in and around the eyes rupture, shooting a thin stream of blood up to 4 feet (1.2 meters) at an attacker.

Regal
horned lizard

Crested porcupine

The stout-bodied crested porcupine is a ground-living creature. It feeds on plant material, such as roots, bulbs, tubers, fruit, and bark.

The spotted skunk stands on its hands and lifts its back legs to spray foul-smelling musk at a predator with great accuracy — up to 15 feet away (4.6 meters)!

Spotted skunk

GOD GAVE SOME USUALLY PEACEFUL ANIMALS UNUSUAL WAYS OF PROTECTING THEMSELVES FROM PREDATORS.

God gave the regal horned lizard a bizarre way of protecting itself. The lizard can squirt jets of stinging blood from its eyes at the mouth and eyes of a tormentor. The African crested porcupine has long, sharp spines on its back and tail. When a predator approaches, the porcupine rattles the hollow quills on its tail as a warning. If that fails, the porcupine will charge backward to drive the spines into its enemy. The skunk can spray a strong-smelling fluid from two pouches beneath its tail to cause temporary blindness and stop a predator from breathing for a few seconds while it escapes.

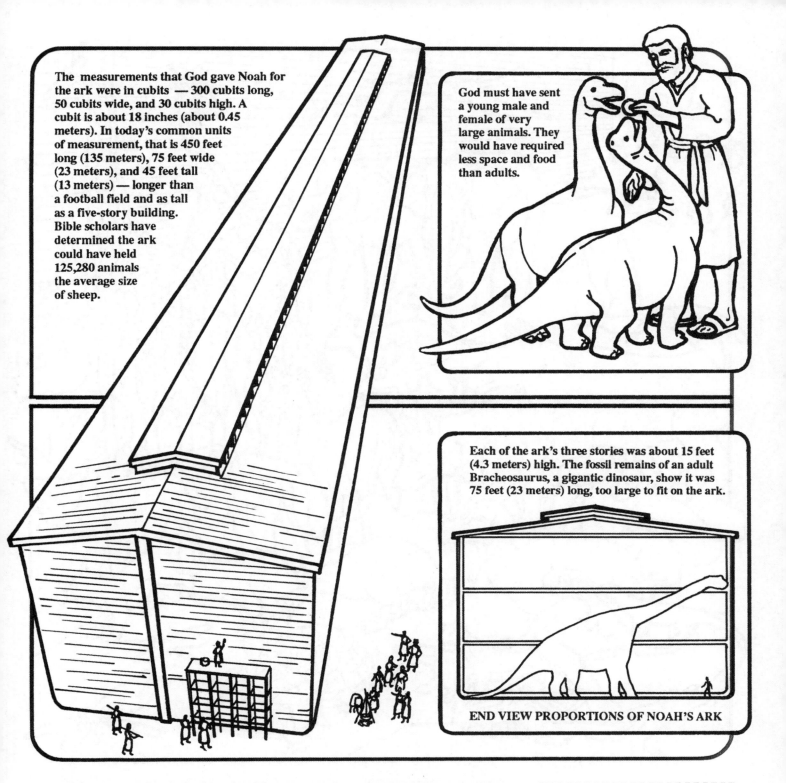

The measurements that God gave Noah for the ark were in cubits — 300 cubits long, 50 cubits wide, and 30 cubits high. A cubit is about 18 inches (about 0.45 meters). In today's common units of measurement, that is 450 feet long (135 meters), 75 feet wide (23 meters), and 45 feet tall (13 meters) — longer than a football field and as tall as a five-story building. Bible scholars have determined the ark could have held 125,280 animals the average size of sheep.

God must have sent a young male and female of very large animals. They would have required less space and food than adults.

Each of the ark's three stories was about 15 feet (4.3 meters) high. The fossil remains of an adult Bracheosaurus, a gigantic dinosaur, show it was 75 feet (23 meters) long, too large to fit on the ark.

END VIEW PROPORTIONS OF NOAH'S ARK

GOD MADE PLANS TO SAVE ANIMAL LIFE WHEN HE DECIDED TO DESTROY THE EARTH WITH A GREAT FLOOD.

The sin-filled earth became so corrupt and filled with violence, God determined to send a world-destroying cataclysm — a flood in which "all flesh" (both animals and mankind) would perish. Only those animals and people aboard a huge ark, built by a man named Noah, who "found grace in the eyes of the Lord," would be saved (Gen. 6:5-13). God told Noah the exact size the ark needed to be to house all the animals He would send to board it (Gen. 6:14-22). The ark was enormous, more than large enough to hold "every sort" of animal God had created along with feed to last for more than a year.

GOD DIRECTED ANIMAL PAIRS, MALE AND FEMALE, TO THE ARK SHORTLY BEFORE THE GREAT FLOOD BEGAN.

God commanded Noah to gather all the plant food his family and the animals would need during their long stay on the ark. But Noah did not have to travel throughout the pre-flood world to gather pairs of every land-dwelling animal kind. Noah merely waited at the ark, and the animals came to him. God selected and sent to Noah "to keep them alive" those animals best-suited to survive and have offspring in the post-flood world (Gen. 6:19-22). God had a purpose for every "kind" of creature He created, and He intended for all the kinds to be preserved aboard the ark with Noah's family.

Pairs made up of male cattle, bulls, and female cattle, cows, were among the "clean" animal kinds God sent to the waiting Noah at the ark.

OF "CLEAN" KINDS OF BEASTS AND BIRDS, GOD SENT SEVEN, THREE PAIRS AND A SINGLE CREATURE, TO NOAH.

The "clean" kinds of beasts (Gen. 7:2, 3) were most likely those that would be especially beneficial after the flood, domesticated animals that live in close harmony with mankind. Perhaps God preserved three pairs of these animals, male and female, to allow for greater variety within the "kind" for breeding purposes. God also sent seven of each bird kind to the ark. "And they went in unto Noah into the ark, two and two of all flesh, wherein is the breath of life." Then God shut the ark's door. And all of the earth's land animals died in the flood, except for those within the ark (Gen. 7:15-23).

The seventh one of the cattle kind was brought to the altar for sacrifice along with one of all the other clean beasts and birds. Pleased with Noah's faith and the sacrificial offerings, God set His rainbow in the clouds — a sign that He never again would send a worldwide flood.

AFTER 371 DAYS IN THE ARK, NOAH, HIS FAMILY, AND ALL THE ANIMALS CAME OUT OF IT TO A CHANGED EARTH.

During the 53 weeks Noah had been aboard the ark, the great flood of "the fountains of the deep" and "the waters above the firmament" destroyed everything. The world that once was no longer existed, and nothing would have been familiar to Noah; but he was thankful that God had mercifully delivered his family from the evil of the pre-flood world and saved the ark's inhabitants. Noah built an altar to make a burnt offering to God — for He had provided Noah with the seventh, single representative of every clean beast and every clean fowl to be used for sacrificial purposes (Gen. 8:20).

After the flood, the land was barren of vegetation. At first, Noah's family and animals that stayed near them probably continued to eat food remaining from provisions that had been stored aboard the ark. Plant life was re-established as seeds and cuttings buried in the soil sprouted, but Noah and his sons must have planted crops as soon as possible, using cattle to till the earth.

Rather than spreading out to repopulate the entire earth as God wished, mankind left the forbidding region of Ararat where the ark landed and journeyed together to the fertile plains of Shinar. There they built a city known as Babel and a great tower. Displeased, God confounded their language. Unable to understand one another's speech, people fled Babel — some probably using cattle to help them move away.

CATTLE, A GREAT HELP TO MEN AFTER THE FLOOD, TRAVELED WITH THEM AS THEY SPREAD OUT OVER THE EARTH.

Following the flood, divine permission was given to mankind to eat animal flesh, and God put a fear and dread (terror) of man in animals (Gen. 9:2-4). This was actually for man's benefit as predatory, carnivorous appetites developed in more and more large animals. Plants growing in the flood-eroded earth evidently could give neither man nor every beast all they needed for proper nutrition. Noah's family must have depended upon cattle to help them raise crops; they may have depended upon cattle for food — eating meat for the first time. When people left Babel, no doubt some families took domesticated cattle with them.

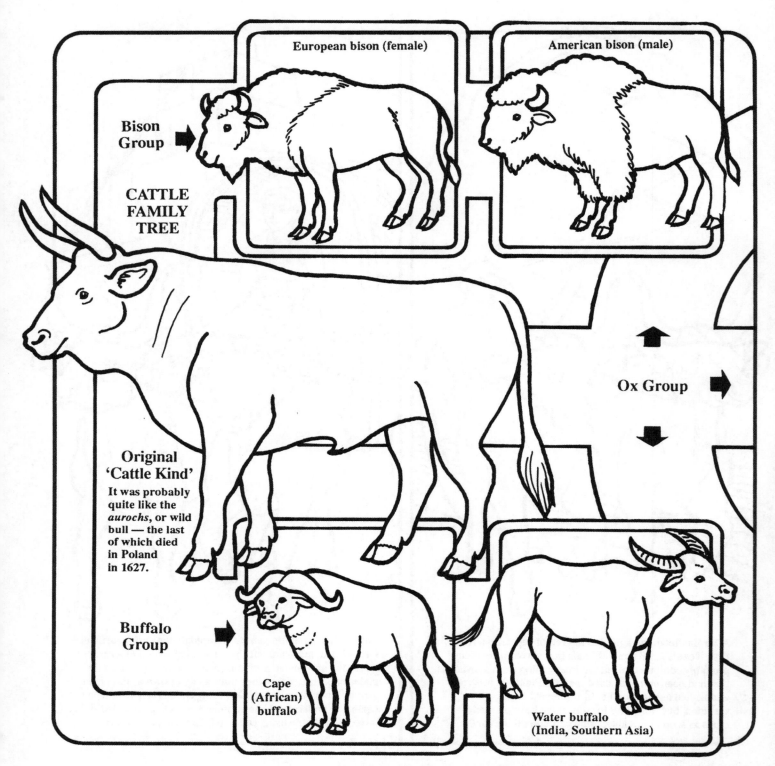

CATTLE FAMILY TREE

Bison Group →

European bison (female)

American bison (male)

Ox Group →

Original 'Cattle Kind'

It was probably quite like the *aurochs*, or wild bull — the last of which died in Poland in 1627.

Buffalo Group →

Cape (African) buffalo

Water buffalo (India, Southern Asia)

ALL OF THE VARIOUS TYPES OF CATTLE IN THE WORLD TODAY CAME FROM THE THREE PAIRS SAVED IN THE ARK.

The original cattle kind made by God in the beginning was genetically much richer than present descendants. God placed the possibilities for great variation within the genes of the first cattle, but there was probably little noticeable difference in the three pairs He sent to the ark. Great diversification took place rapidly, however, with the migration and dispersal of cattle kind from Babel. Taken with them by men whom God scattered abroad throughout the earth (Gen. 11:8), small groups of cattle developed special, unique characteristics when they were separated and isolated from others of their kind.

Yak (Tibet)

A cave painting of the aurochs, the ancestor of European domesticated cattle.

Zebu (Humped Indian cattle)

Jersey

Holstein

Guernsey DAIRY CATTLE Ayrshire

SOME MODERN BREEDS OF CATTLE

BEEF CATTLE

Angus

Shorthorn

Santa Gertrudis

Hereford

SPECIAL TYPES OF CATTLE WITH DESIRED TRAITS HAVE BEEN DEVELOPED THROUGH SELECTIVE BREEDING.

The spread of cattle across the world was not only by human assistance, but also by natural migration. Some cattle remained domesticated, but others escaped from their owners and lived in the wild, migrating to areas where they could thrive. It was God's will that all the animals, including cattle, "may breed abundantly in the earth, and be fruitful, and multiply upon the earth" (Gen. 8:17). As cattle multiplied, men noticed that some gave more milk than others and that the meat of some was better than others. Through selective breeding, such desired characteristics were brought out.

25

The favorite drink of Tibetans is hot tea mixed with yak butter.

SOME TYPES OF CATTLE ARE AT HOME IN EARTH'S HOT REGIONS; OTHER CATTLE ARE AT HOME IN COLD AREAS.

Plant fossils show that temperatures must have been mild worldwide in the beginning. After the flood, the earth began to have great temperature variations from pole to pole. In all the hot wet lands of southeast Asia, the main food crop is rice. There, the farmer uses a water buffalo to pull his plough through the muddy soil to turn it before he plants the rice. In the high, cold Himalayan mountains, the people of Tibet use yaks for carrying heavy loads. The yak's long hair is used to weave warm clothing, blankets, and tents. The yak's milk is turned into butter, and its dried dung is used as fuel.

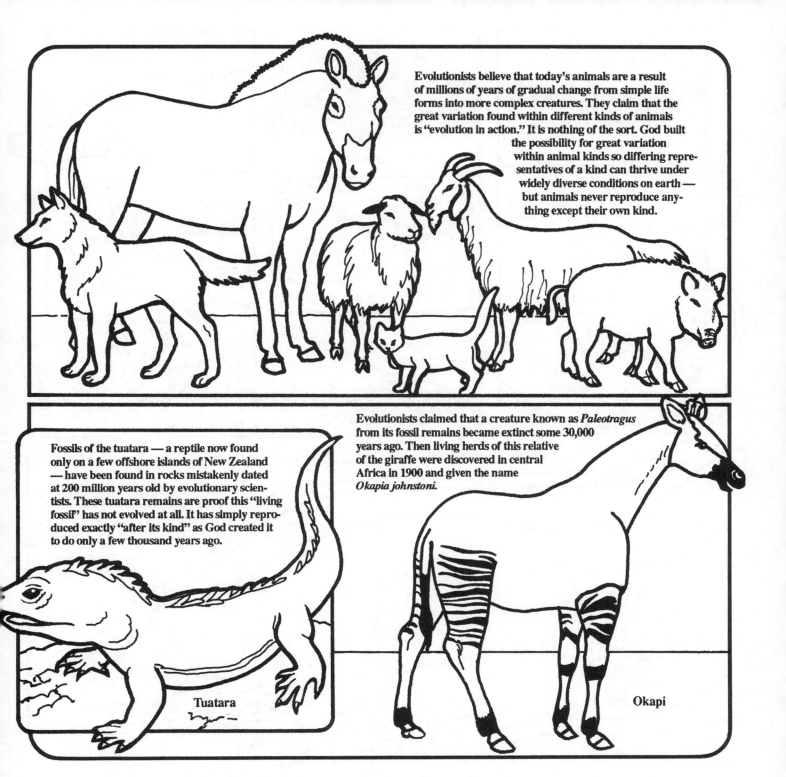

Evolutionists believe that today's animals are a result of millions of years of gradual change from simple life forms into more complex creatures. They claim that the great variation found within different kinds of animals is "evolution in action." It is nothing of the sort. God built the possibility for great variation within animal kinds so differing representatives of a kind can thrive under widely diverse conditions on earth — but animals never reproduce anything except their own kind.

Fossils of the tuatara — a reptile now found only on a few offshore islands of New Zealand — have been found in rocks mistakenly dated at 200 million years old by evolutionary scientists. These tuatara remains are proof this "living fossil" has not evolved at all. It has simply reproduced exactly "after its kind" as God created it to do only a few thousand years ago.

Evolutionists claimed that a creature known as *Paleotragus* from its fossil remains became extinct some 30,000 years ago. Then living herds of this relative of the giraffe were discovered in central Africa in 1900 and given the name *Okapia johnstoni*.

Tuatara

Okapi

LIKE CATTLE, ADDITIONAL ANIMAL KINDS SHOW GREAT VARIATION. OTHER CREATURES DISPLAY LITTLE VARIATION.

From the representatives of animal kinds aboard the ark, great variation has developed from all the genes that God originally put there. For example, all dog breeds from tiny Chihuahuas to the heavy Saint Bernard have come from the original wolf-like dog stock. On the other hand, there are creatures known as "living fossils," such as the tuatara (the only living survivor of an otherwise extinct group of reptiles known as *rhynchocephalians*, or "beakheads") and the okapi, that show little variation compared to preserved remains of their kind likely fossilized as a result of the great flood.

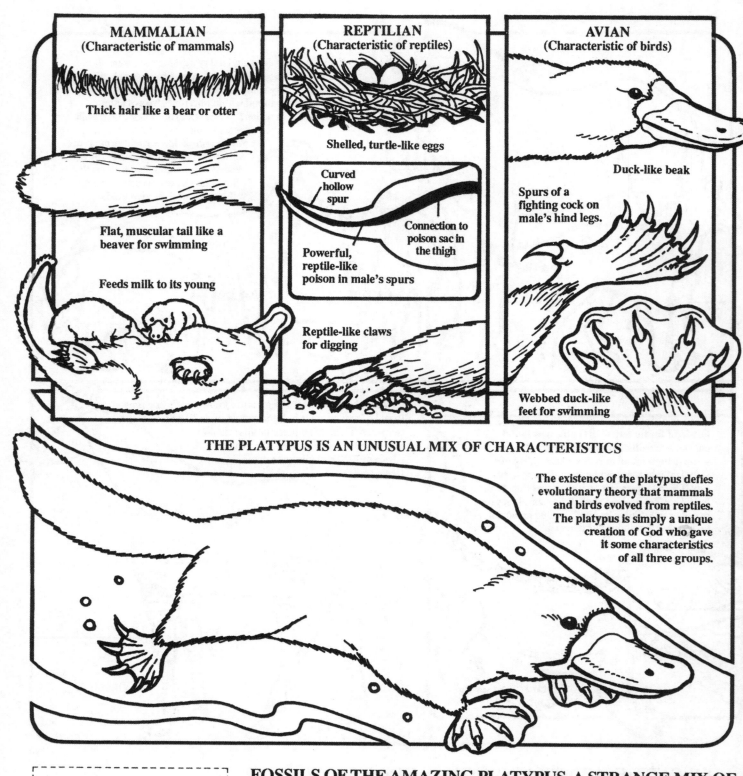

MAMMALIAN
(Characteristic of mammals)

Thick hair like a bear or otter

Flat, muscular tail like a beaver for swimming

Feeds milk to its young

REPTILIAN
(Characteristic of reptiles)

Shelled, turtle-like eggs

Curved hollow spur

Connection to poison sac in the thigh

Powerful, reptile-like poison in male's spurs

Reptile-like claws for digging

AVIAN
(Characteristic of birds)

Duck-like beak

Spurs of a fighting cock on male's hind legs.

Webbed duck-like feet for swimming

THE PLATYPUS IS AN UNUSUAL MIX OF CHARACTERISTICS

The existence of the platypus defies evolutionary theory that mammals and birds evolved from reptiles. The platypus is simply a unique creation of God who gave it some characteristics of all three groups.

FOSSILS OF THE AMAZING PLATYPUS, A STRANGE MIX OF ANIMAL CHARACTERISTICS, SHOW IT HAS NOT EVOLVED.

Just because the platypus, a mammal, is found today only in Australia, evolutionists believed it evolved there from reptiles. However, fossil remains found in Australia in 1984, (wrongly) dated 110 million years old, display no evolutionary progress at all. Then in 1991 a fossil platypus tooth was found in Patagonia, near the tip of South America. This shows the platypus may well have reached many other parts of the world in journeying from Ararat — generations traveling for many years over once-existing land bridges or on floating islands of matted vegetation — to survive only in Australia.

Llama

Indian elephant

People called *mahouts* trap wild elephants and train them. A trained elephant learns to respond to over 30 commands which it never forgets.

GOD CREATED ANIMALS THAT ARE VERY USEFUL TO MANKIND TODAY IN DIFFERENT PLACES ON EARTH.

Llamas have been useful to man for many centuries in the mountains of South America. Sure-footed and very strong for their size, the male llamas are perfect pack animals — carrying heavy loads many miles a day over rough ground. The female is highly valued for her wool, milk, meat, and hide. Elephants are a great help to people in southern Asia by doing heavy labor. They plow farmlands at half the cost of operating tractors. Elephants effortlessly fell huge trees, pull massive loads, and carry logs in the deep, dense tropical forests where modern machinery cannot operate.

The Wise Men

Camel

Jesus

Donkey

Jesus' mother Mary likely rode a donkey to Bethlehem, and Jesus was carried by one into Jerusalem as crowds cheered.

GOD CREATED ANIMALS THAT WERE VERY USEFUL IN TO PEOPLE IN BIBLE LANDS, JUST AS THEY ARE TODAY.

For at least four thousand years, camels have carried heavy loads and people across the dry deserts of the Middle East. God gave the camel big feet to keep it from sinking into the sand, and it can go without a drink for more than a week. The wise men probably rode camels when they brought gifts to the Christ child. The donkey is raised as a farm, pack, and riding animal. It can survive in places where other creatures cannot on coarse grass and weeds. Very strong and hard-working for its small size, the donkey easily carries loads of over 250 pounds (113.6 kilograms).

In the future, God will restore the harmony that existed between humans and animals in Eden. Read Hosea 2:18 and Ezekiel 34:25.

Jesus is the Good Shepherd

When Christ returns there will be peace between the lion and the lamb.

Read Isaiah 11:6-9

David, the shepherd boy

Read Samuel 17:34-37

SHEEP WERE IMPORTANT TO PEOPLE IN BIBLE TIMES, AND SHEPHERDS PROTECTED THEM FROM FIERCE PREDATORS.

Sheep were valuable to people in the Bible. Their wool was woven into clothing and they were eaten and used for sacrifice. Gentle creatures, sheep were easy prey for predators like lions and wolves, but a good shepherd would protect them with his very life. King David, remembering his youth as a shepherd boy, wrote, "The Lord is my shepherd" in the beautiful Twenty-third Psalm. God compares His people to sheep in the Bible (Psa. 100:3, Isa. 53:6). And Jesus called himself "the Good Shepherd," who not only guides His sheep but also dies for them (John 10:1-21).

"A righteous man regardeth the life of his beast."
— Proverbs 12:10

BEING GOOD STEWARDS OF GOD'S WORLD BY HAVING PROPER CONCERN FOR ANIMALS IS IMPORTANT.

God placed animals under man's dominion (Gen. 1:26-28), and He expects responsible stewardship, not unkindness or cruelty toward animals. Even though mankind can use animals for work, food, clothing, and other useful purposes, they should be respected as God's creatures. Always treat the animals God has placed in your care with kindness and consideration (Deut. 25:4). Give them nourishing food on a regular feeding schedule. Keep them clean and well-groomed. Domesticated animals must be vaccinated to protect them from diseases. Be a good steward and pet owner.